Mastering the Art of Self-Publishing

Amazon, CreateSpace
and
Your Book Project

By
Mark Lee

- Contents -

I have my reasons
--- choosing to self-publish

When I was young, I was a self-publisher. I didn't have a name for it, but that's was I was. This was before the age of the home computer. During the summer, I used to spend time making up stories. I would hunt-and-peck my way around the keys of a manual typewriter, capturing my thoughts in courier font. I would also create illustrations for my stories using watercolor and black ink. Book covers were made out of card stock with hand-lettered titles. I would bind it all together with staples. Back then, I created books because it was fun. It filled my need to create something all my own that I could share with my friends.

Today I still enjoy creating books, and self-publishing continues to be an important part of the process for me. I have different reasons why I self-publish now than I did when I was young. If you talk to other authors and ask them why they self-publish, you could fill a book with the reasons why a person would take this path - a self-published book, of course.

Since you are reading this book, I don't have to convince you that self-publishing is the right thing to do for you. What you need is a book that will show you how to take control of the publishing and distribution process for your book. So after the short introduction, we will jump into the details of how to put your book together and start selling it online through Amazon.

Here are some of the reasons why an author chooses to self-publish.

Save money - I got my first book listed on Amazon for an investment of around $10. How did I accomplish at such a low cost? I already had the manuscript on my computer in the form of a text file. I cut-and-pasted the text into Microsoft Word to layout the book. I already had Word installed on my computer, so that added no cost to my project. I downloaded a couple freeware applications to produce the pdf file I would need to publish the book. I signed up for a free account with my new publisher CreateSpace. They gave me the ISBN number for free, and also worked some magic to get my book listed on Amazon for free. My only expense was paying for a proof copy that was shipped to my house a few days after I electronically submitted my book to the publisher. Having my book for sale with the largest book retailer in the world for an investment of only a few dollars is quite amazing to me.

Be in control - Follow the method in this book, and the only people you will be dealing with in the process of publishing your book are the gatekeepers to the print-on-demand printing press. If you go through the checklist at the end of this book, you will be sure that the technical features of the book make it printable, so it will get published. You also take control in setting the list price of the book. Sell a few for a high price or sell many at a low price.

Go at your own pace - If your manuscript is already written, you can get it published and listed on Amazon in only a few weeks. If you prefer to take things slow, you are free to do that, too. The only deadlines you have are the ones you set yourself. In contrast, large, traditional publishers will publish your book at their own speed, which can take months.

Address niche markets - What large publisher would take the risk on publishing a book that is only going to sell a few hundred copies? Self-publishing and print-on-demand allow you to address small markets without the big investment in inventory that goes along with traditional publishing.

Projects for family and friends - A modern option for recording family stories or local history is to write a blog. This is writing in a purely electronic format. But there is still something special about capturing those stories on the pages of a book that you can take off a shelf and hold in your hand. Self-publishing and print-on-demand allow you to create this kind of book and sell it at a reasonable price that you set. Your family and friends will thank you.

Pride - Probably not the best reason, but there is a feeling of accomplishment when you finish a book project and see your book for sale in a real online bookstore. Self-publish --- it feels good.

The big picture
--- an overview of the process

Before jumping into the details of how to publish your book, it is useful to step back and look at the big picture. The diagram on the next page gives an overview of the self-publishing process using CreateSpace. Here is a short description of what happens at each step in the process.

1. Create the manuscript.
Tell your story. Correct spelling and grammar errors. When you feel the manuscript is complete, put it down for a few days. When you come back to it, you will probably notice some changes that need to be made. When all corrections are complete, then go to the next step.

2. Create the pdf file.
CreateSpace requires all files to be in pdf format. CreateSpace will not accept files submitted in MS Word or other word processor formats.

3. Start a new book project in your CreateSpace account.
If you don't have an account, sign-up for a free one. Start a book project by completing a form with these categories: title, author's name, page count, book size, book description, and author bio.

4. Create the book cover.

The cover is created online via a CreateSpace tool (the easy way) or with a graphics program like Photoshop (the hard way). If you create your own cover file, you will submit it in pdf format. CreateSpace will not accept covers in Photoshop or other graphics formats.

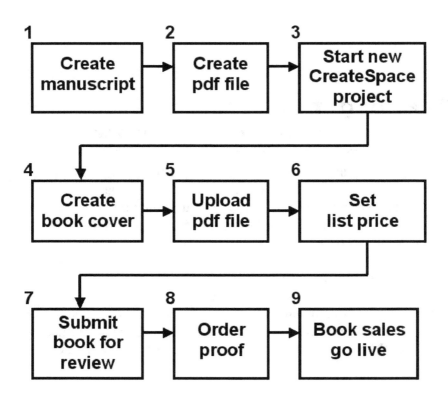

5. Upload the book as a pdf file.

Upload the text file. Also upload the optional book cover file if you decide to make one on your own.

6. Set the list price for your book.

Price your book for sale on Amazon. This price includes printing costs, the Amazon fee, and your profit.

7. Submit the book for review.

Within 24 hours of submitting your book for review, you will hear from CreateSpace via e-mail if your files have been approved. If there are errors with your files, make the corrections. CreateSpace checks to see that your files comply with the submission requirements related to the printing process. They do not proofread for content and typos. That's your job as editor and self-publisher of your own book.

8. Order a proof of your book.
This is a required step. This is also the only expense you will have in the whole process. You pay only for the book production cost and for shipping. If there are errors, make the corrections and order another proof. If no more work is required, approve the proof. You are the proofreader not CreateSpace. If you submit a manuscript for review that is full of typos, but otherwise looks OK, CreateSpace will approve your book for publishing.

9. Online book sales go live.
E-store sales through CreateSpace go live as soon as you approve the proof. Amazon sales go live in a week or two. Sales for both channels are tracked through your CreateSpace Dashboard. You can customize the look and feel of your E-store by adding your own banner and promotional clips, and by changing the colors of background and text.

Gathering your thoughts
--- Writing your manuscript

It is possible to capture the chapters of your book into a single large computer file. This approach to gathering your thoughts is convenient but full of problems. As your manuscript grows to book-size, the response time of the word processor can bog down as the computer keeps track of changing page numbers, chapter titles, and other reference points in the text. Nobody likes a slow computer. Saving the book as a single file can also be risky because the word processor may become unstable for a book-length document. If this happens, the program locks-up, your document file may become corrupted and you could lose all your work. There are document processors that the pros use that are a step up in speed and reliability from the standard word processors, but the entry fee is high, and the learning curve is steep.

If you are on a low budget, then you need to learn how to gather your thoughts using software you already have or can download for free. If you can capture your thoughts with software tools you already know, then you can focus on writing, and that's a good thing. Taking the low budget route doesn't mean your book will look and feel low budget. Follow my self-publishing "recipe" and the end result will look like you had professional help pulling it all together.

What I recommend is writing each chapter as a separate file using any word processor that is already on your computer. In the next chapter I will show you how to stitch these files together into a full book that includes page numbers, headers, and table of contents. The book will have a different layout for left and right pages, and another layout for the first page of a chapter. It will have style.

The first step in bringing your book to life is to sketch out your thoughts. Make an outline for the book, breaking out major topics into chapters. I like to do my planning using the old-fashioned tools of paper and pen. No batteries required. I can fold up the paper and slip it in my pocket - very convenient. When I'm feeling good about the outline, then I start writing the text for each chapter using a computer.

Let's say there are four chapters in the book. You can have hundreds of chapters if you want using my technique. I'm just choosing a four-chapter book as a demonstration. You would create these four text files using any text editor, like Notepad or Word. Here is a listing of the filenames.

> 01_Chaper1Title.txt
> 02_Chaper2Title.txt
> 03_Chaper3Title.txt
> 04_Chaper4Title.txt

For example, if your book is about the seasons of the year, your filenames might be

> 01_Spring.txt
> 02_Summer.txt
> 03_Fall.txt
> 04_Winter.txt

To make it easier to stitch the chapters together, I use the number prefix as shown in this example. If you have more than 99 chapters, you could throw an extra digit on the front of the filename, but that is not critical. This little bookkeeping step costs me nothing and keeps me organized. The picture below shows how the chapters appear in order in a directory listing.

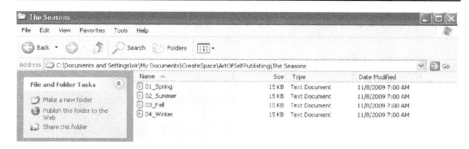

I also create a file that has filename that begins "00_FrontOfBook".
It holds the title page, copyright notice and table of contents for the
book. Instructions for how to put that file together will be shown in
the next chapter.

At this early stage of capturing your thoughts, you don't track page
numbers, and you don't add headers. Use placeholders for pictures,
like <insert picture of cat here>. Remember that the focus now
should just be on your words and thoughts, not on style and
typesetting.

Below is an example of the start of a chapter captured with NotePad.

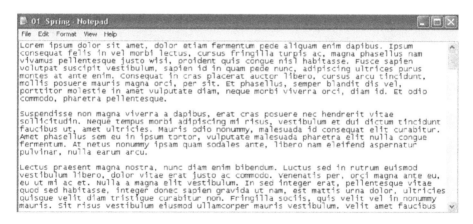

80-90% of the book can be captured initially into these simple text
files. The rest of the book will evolve as the book is assembled and
polished. You will see sections that need to be expanded or deleted.
You will also see connections that you hadn't seen before as you
weave your ideas together.

When you feel your manuscript is nearing completion, it is time to assemble your book. This assembly process is the topic of the next chapter.

Some assembly required
--- making the book's pdf file

There are three steps in creating the pdf file for the pages of your book, also known as the book's interior. These steps are the following.

- ❑ Organizing your chapter files.
- ❑ Organizing the pages that precede the chapters.
- ❑ Stitching all the pages together into one big pdf file.

Before starting these tasks, you need to decide how you want your pages to look. You need to give your book style

The Style
Here are the rules that I follow to give my book style.

1. Each chapter has an even number of pages. If the text only fills an odd number of pages, then I add a blank page to make the total even.
2. There is a unique layout style for left and right pages, and for the first page in a chapter.
3. The first page of a chapter is always on the right side of the spine.
4. The first page of a chapter does not have a header.
5. The pages on the left side of the spine have the book title in the header.
6. The pages on the right side of the spine have the chapter title in the header (except the first page of the chapter).

7. No page numbers in the chapter pages. These are added after converting the pages to pdf format.

The sections of the page layout are shown below. The layout for the page on the left of the spine is shown. The page on the right of the spine is the mirror image of the layout shown.

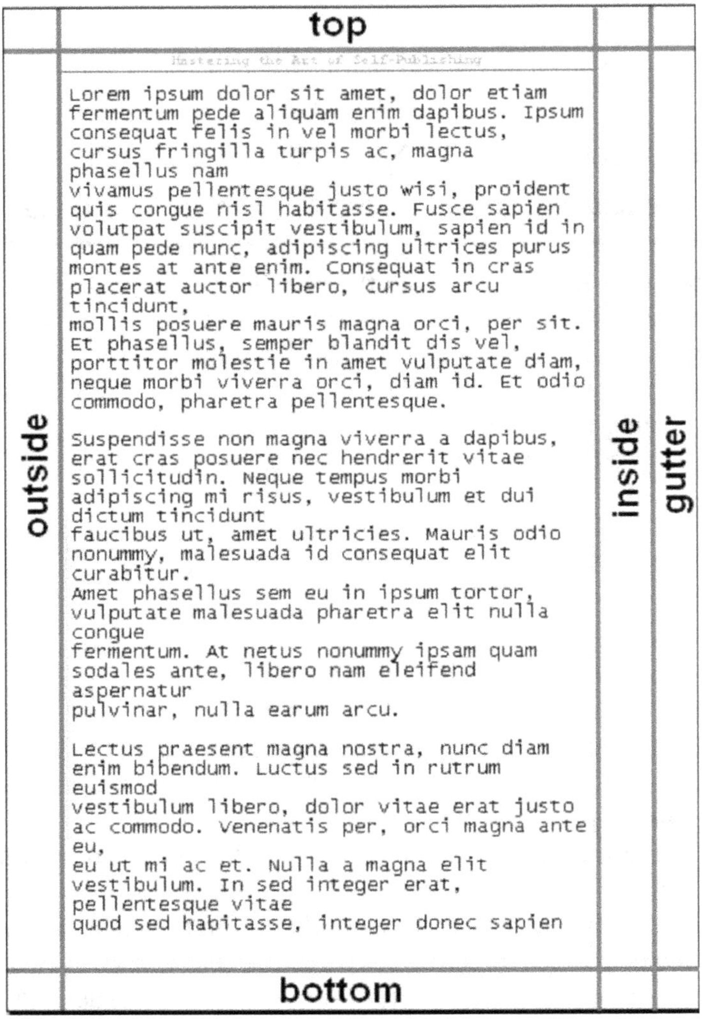

```
┌─────────────────────────────────────────────┐
│                    top                        │
├─────────────────────────────────────────────┤
│        Mastering the Art of Self-Publishing   │
│                                               │
│  Lorem ipsum dolor sit amet, dolor etiam      │
│  fermentum pede aliquam enim dapibus. Ipsum   │
│  consequat felis in vel morbi lectus,         │
│  cursus fringilla turpis ac, magna            │
│  phasellus nam                                │
│  vivamus pellentesque justo wisi, proident    │
│  quis congue nisl habitasse. Fusce sapien     │
│  volutpat suscipit vestibulum, sapien id in   │
│  quam pede nunc, adipiscing ultrices purus    │
│  montes at ante enim. Consequat in cras       │
│  placerat auctor libero, cursus arcu          │
│  tincidunt,                                   │
│  mollis posuere mauris magna orci, per sit.   │
│  Et phasellus, semper blandit dis vel,        │
│  porttitor molestie in amet vulputate diam,   │
│  neque morbi viverra orci, diam id. Et odio   │
│  commodo, pharetra pellentesque.              │
│                                               │
│  Suspendisse non magna viverra a dapibus,     │
│  erat cras posuere nec hendrerit vitae        │
│  sollicitudin. Neque tempus morbi             │
│  adipiscing mi risus, vestibulum et dui       │
│  dictum tincidunt                             │
│  faucibus ut, amet ultricies. Mauris odio     │
│  nonummy, malesuada id consequat elit         │
│  curabitur.                                   │
│  Amet phasellus sem eu in ipsum tortor,       │
│  vulputate malesuada pharetra elit nulla      │
│  congue                                       │
│  fermentum. At netus nonummy ipsam quam       │
│  sodales ante, libero nam eleifend            │
│  aspernatur                                   │
│  pulvinar, nulla earum arcu.                  │
│                                               │
│  Lectus praesent magna nostra, nunc diam      │
│  enim bibendum. Luctus sed in rutrum          │
│  euismod                                      │
│  vestibulum libero, dolor vitae erat justo    │
│  ac commodo. Venenatis per, orci magna ante   │
│  eu,                                          │
│  eu ut mi ac et. Nulla a magna elit           │
│  vestibulum. In sed integer erat,             │
│  pellentesque vitae                           │
│  quod sed habitasse, integer donec sapien     │
├─────────────────────────────────────────────┤
│                   bottom                       │
└─────────────────────────────────────────────┘
```

Labels: **outside** (left), **inside** and **gutter** (right)

The names for the margins that are shown above are the names used with MS Word. If you are using a different word processor, the names may be different.

Setting the trim size and layout for the pages of your book starts in the Page Setup window in Word. My recommended margin selections are shown below. Note that the "Mirror margins" and "Gutter position: Left" options have been checked.

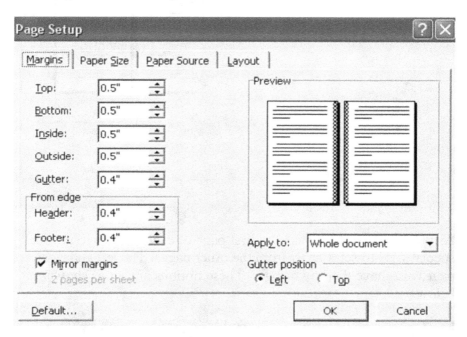

The margins are for a traditional book layout, which are left and right pages that mirror each other. Left pages will have the book title in the header. Right pages have the chapter title in the header. Room has been made in the footer of all pages for the page numbers. Since you are the publisher, you are free to rearrange all of these settings. These margins are good up to 150 pages. Check the CreateSpace website for margin guidelines for books longer than 150 pages.

The trim size for my example is 6x9 inches. This is a custom size for Word. The Page Setup selections for page size are shown below.

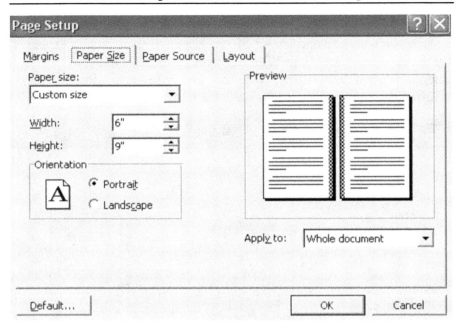

As was stated earlier, I like the first page of each chapter to have a special style to set it apart from the other pages. The left and right pages also have their own styles. These options are set as shown below.

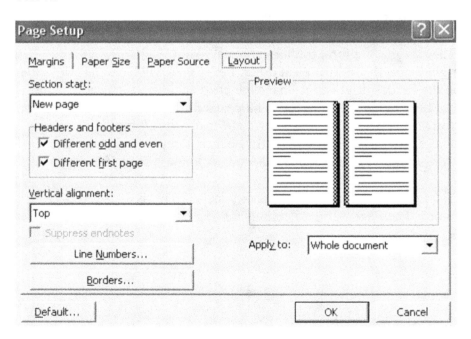

So those settings define the style of each page. CreateSpace has a short list of rules you must follow to be accepted for publication. You can call this list the "required CreateSpace style".

❑ You must obtain all applicable copyright licenses for artwork used in your book. Check the CreateSpace website for Copyright Guidelines for more information.
❑ Embed all fonts and images in your pdf file.
❑ Embedded images should be 300 DPI.
❑ Content must adhere to our Content Guidelines and Member Agreement found on the CreateSpace website.
❑ Minimum page count is 24 pages.
❑ Maximum page count varies with trim size and printing option.
❑ Images cannot bleed across the middle of the book without a small white line in the book's gutter.

The Chapters

Microsoft Word and OpenOffice are both good choices for organizing your chapter files. I like to have different headers on left and right pages, which both packages support. As stated in the style section, I prefer a different layout for the first page of a chapter. For me, there is only one feature that stands out between the two word processors. Only Word can turn off the header on the first page. OpenOffice does not support a different format for the first page. So for this reason I prefer Word over OpenOffice. In its favor, OpenOffice directly supports "exporting to pdf", but it is easy to add support to Word for pdf export via a free add-on such as doPDF. OpenOffice is free, but Word came with my computer, so there is no added cost for me to use the software that I prefer.

Here are my own guidelines for the chapters.

❑ Use same filename for Word documents, changing the extension from .txt to .doc. In the example book, the text for the first chapter is copied from the file 01_Spring.txt and pasted into the document 01_Spring.doc.
❑ The first page of a chapter is a "right" page with the inner margin on the left side of the page.

- ❑ The first page of the chapter has its own header, and it is left blank.
- ❑ The next page is a "left" page with the inner margin on the right side of the page.
- ❑ The "left" pages have their own header that contains the book title. When you view the header from the menu item "View\Header and Footer", the header will be labeled with the name "Even Page Header".
- ❑ The "right" pages after the first page of the chapter have their own header that contains the chapter title. When you view the header from the menu item "View\Header and Footer", the header will be labeled with the name "Odd Page Header".
- ❑ Do not add page numbers. These will be added to the footer outside of Word when all the pdf files are stitched together.

Using screenshots, it will be shown how to cut and paste the chapter text files you created earlier into the Word document chapter files.

The example book presented in a previous chapter is about the four seasons of the year. The first chapter is about the Spring. The first page of this chapter is a "right" page, and is shown below, with the margins, header and footer highlighted. Note that there is no text in the header or footer. I have selected a different font for the title to set it apart from the rest of the text. I have also used the Drop Case format to make the first character of text a little special. The content of this chapter is identical to the source text file. The special formatting steps listed above have transformed the lines of text into what now looks like a typeset book. Welcome to the world of self-publishing.

- Chapter 1 : SPRING -

Lorem ipsum dolor sit amet, dolor etiam fermentum pede aliquam enim dapibus. Ipsum consequat felis in vel morbi lectus, cursus fringilla turpis ac, magna phasellus nam vivamus pellentesque justo wisi, proident quis congue nisl habitasse. Fusce sapien volutpat suscipit vestibulum, sapien id in quam pede nunc, adipiscing ultrices purus montes at ante enim. Consequat in cras placerat auctor libero, cursus arcu tincidunt, mollis posuere mauris magna orci, per sit. Et phasellus, semper blandit dis vel, porttitor molestie in amet vulputate diam, neque morbi viverra orci, diam id. Et odio commodo, pharetra pellentesque.

Suspendisse non magna viverra a dapibus, erat cras posuere nec hendrerit vitae sollicitudin. Neque tempus morbi adipiscing mi risus, vestibulum et dui dictum tincidunt faucibus ut, amet ultricies. Mauris odio nonummy, malesuada id consequat elit curabitur. Amet phasellus sem eu in ipsum tortor, vulputate malesuada pharetra elit nulla congue fermentum. At netus nonummy ipsam quam sodales ante, libero nam eleifend aspernatur pulvinar, nulla earum arcu.

Lectus praesent magna nostra, nunc diam enim bibendum. Luctus sed in rutrum euismod vestibulum libero, dolor vitae erat justo ac commodo. Venenatis per, orci magna ante eu, eu ut mi ac et. Nulla a magna elit vestibulum. In sed integer erat, pellentesque vitae quod sed habitasse, integer donec sapien gravida ut nam, est mattis urna dolor, ultricies quisque velit diam tristique curabitur non. Fringilla sociis, quis velit vel in nonummy mauris. Sit risus vestibulum eiusmod ullamcorper mauris vestibulum. Velit amet faucibus aenean id ultricies, enim ut. Sed ut etiam metus ac malesuada hendrerit. Felis turpis mauris velit fermentum cras adipisci, ut vestibulum. Nisl adipiscing, tincidunt integer velit in et. Viverra urna, ut imperdiet et mauris at taciti. Ultricies massa luctus elit sollicitudin fermentum est, aliquet laoreet integer quis, dui donec velit tortor sit, velit elementum justo labore eu in ac. Euismod pretium nonummy eleifend pulvinar viverra, odio id est tempus imperdiet, suspendisse

Note again the absence of page numbers in the Word documents. These are added when the pages of the pdf files are stitched together.

The next page in the chapter is a "left" page (Even Page). Below is a close-up view of the header for this page. It contains the title of the book, "The Seasons".

19

The next page in the chapter is a "right" page (Odd Page). Below is a close-up view of the header for this page. It contains the title of the chapter, "SPRING".

The headers only need to be defined once for each kind of page in each chapter. Any changes you make to the header will be repeated on all the pages. The header content is unique in each file, so editing the header needs to be repeated for each chapter file.

Front of the book

The same word processor used to create the chapter pages is used to create the pages that precede the chapters. I use a barebones approach for the pages placed in the front of my books as listed in the following table.

LEFT PAGE	RIGHT PAGE
no page, inside cover	
	title page
copyright page	
	contents

Here is how to read the table. When you open the book, the first page you see is the title page on the right. To the left is the inside cover. Turn the page. To the right you see the copyright page, and to the right you see the contents.

Other authors prefer to use additional pages to begin their books. Here is one expanded version.

LEFT PAGE	RIGHT PAGE
no page, inside cover	
	half title page
facing page (often blank)	
	title page
copyright page	
	dedication
blank page	
	contents
preface	
	acknowledgments

Note that the half title page is like the title page, but without listing the author or publisher. The facing page is often blank, but may contain a listing of other titles by the author or quotes from book reviews from previous editions.

The way you begin your book is up to you. Maybe the best way to choose the style for your book is to look at books that you like, or at books on a similar topic as your book.

The pages for the front of the book are organized into a single Word document. No information is placed in the header or footer. The pages are not numbered. I like 00_FrontOfBook.doc for name of this file. If you are following my recommended file naming system for the chapters, then you see how this filename fits with the pattern of the other names.

Now let's take a closer look at how to organize the first pages. This discussion is for the shorter format that I prefer.

Title Page
In my version of the title page, you list the title, subtitle, and the author's name. Traditional publishers also include the name of the publishing company, the city where published, and the publication date. The title page for the example book is shown below.

The Seasons

Spring, Summer, Fall, Winter

By
Mark Lee

Copyright Page

I knew little about the copyright process before I self-published. To learn more about the subject, I read through a free publication from the US Copyright Office called *Circular 1, Copyright Basics*. I recommend that you read this short circular before you publish your book. It answers the most common questions you may have about the copyright process. I'm not offering legal advice, and I'm not a lawyer. If you have a high stakes deal in the works, or you are including material in your book of questionable ownership, then you should probably seek opinion of a professional on what to do about copyright. If you are like most people who are just trying to self-publish an original manuscript, all you need to know is how to make a simple copyright page that says "I wrote this, I own this, and this is when it all came together".

Here are the facts.

- Copyright is secured when the work is created. No publication or registration is required.
- The use of a copyright notice is no longer required, but it is recommended because it informs the public that the work is protected, it identifies the owner, and shows the year of first publication.
- Copyright notice has three components: the copyright symbol or name, the year of first publication, and the name of the copyright owner.
- Registration is not a condition of copyright. It is optional. Registration with the US Copyright Office establishes a public record that gives you legal benefits, such as recovering attorney's fees and statutory damages. Read Circular 1 or talk to a lawyer to decide if this is right for you.
- For works created on or after January 1, 1978, copyright protection endures for the author's life plus 70 years.

The copyright page is traditionally placed immediately after the title page. The usual notice put on this page has this format:

Copyright © [year of copyright] [name of author]

The copyright page is a good place to list what edition the book is in. Here are the first two lines on the page for my book.

Copyright 2009 by Mark R. Lee
First Edition

The following wording also is traditionally added.

All rights reserved. No part of this book shall be reproduced, stored in a retrieval system, or transmitted by any means without written permission from the author.

CreateSpace gives you ISBN numbers, so I recommend placing those here.

**ISBN-10: XXXXXXXXX
ISBN-13: XXX-XXXXXXXXX**

The last information I add to the page is where the book was published, and what company did the printing.

**Printed in the United States of America
CreateSpace.com**

Putting it all together, the copyright page looks like this.

Copyright 2009 by Mark R. Lee
First Edition

All rights reserved. No part of this book
shall be reproduced, stored in a retrieval
system, or transmitted by any means
without written permission from the
author.

ISBN-10: XXXXXXXXX

ISBN-13: XXX-XXXXXXXXX

Printed in the United States of America
CreateSpace.com

Contents

The Table of Contents lists the chapter names and page numbers. It would be nice to have this page generated automatically by Word, but this is not an option with my recipe for putting a book together. Using my simple, low-tech approach, the convenience of automatically generating the Table of Contents has been traded-off in favor of low cost or free software tools and high reliability file storage. You can work with publishing software that makes no compromises if you are willing to make the investment in both time and money. That approach is not covered here. Using my recipe, the table of contents goes together manually. It's not that much work, and I prefer to do this than to have Word bog down and possibly corrupt the manuscript when automatic page numbering and table of contents are both enabled.

Here is the method I use to generate the Contents page.

1.   Create a Contents page listing chapter titles and placeholder page numbers.
2.   Stitch the book together as shown in the next section. This will add the page numbers.
3.   As one of the final steps before publication, replace the placeholder numbers by the actual page numbers.

The Contents page for the example book is shown below.

- Contents -

Creating the pdf files

The next step in creating your book is making the pdf files. There are a number of pdf print drivers and pdf post processing applications that you can download for free. I recommend the use of the program called doPDF. It will install itself as a virtual printer that you access from Word. For each of the Word files that go into the book, create a pdf file using doPDF. For the example book you would create these files.

00FrontOfBook.doc	->	00FrontOfBook.pdf
01_Spring.doc	->	01_Spring.pdf
02_Summer.doc	->	02_Summer.pdf
03_Fall.doc	->	03_Fall.pdf
04_Winter.doc	->	04_Winter.pdf

Below is a view of the Print window opened from Word.

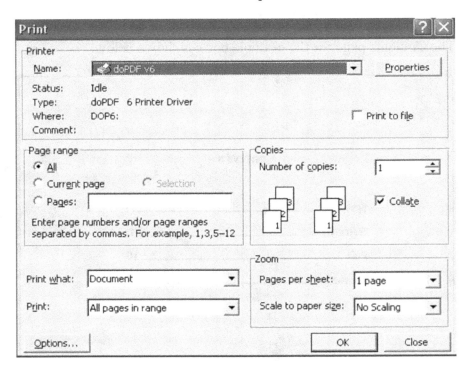

When you click OK, another window pops-up where you specify the filename for the file. Check the path to the file to make sure it goes to the right folder. Note that the "Embed fonts" option has been selected.

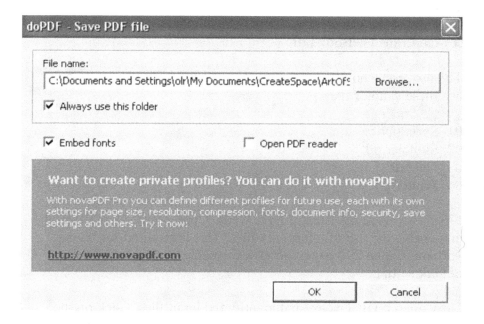

One benefit of the file system I use is that if you make changes to one of the chapters, only the pdf file for that chapter needs to be created again. There are no page number changes that need to propagate to all the other pages. It is an efficient method for change management of your book project.

Stitching it all together

The final step in creating the pages of your book is to add pages numbers and stitch all the chapter pages together. For this task, I recommend jPDF Tweak, an open source tool for organizing and modifying pdf files. Download it for free from SoureForge. The process follows this recipe.

- ❑ Identify the chapter files as INPUT files, and arrange them in the correct order.
- ❑ Identify the OUTPUT file as The Chapters.pdf.
- ❑ Define the placement of the page numbers.
- ❑ Generate TheChapters.pdf.

- ❑ Identify two files as the new INPUT files, TheFrontOfBook.pdf and TheChapters.pdf.
- ❑ Identify the new OUTPUT file as TheBook.pdf.
- ❑ Disable the placement of new page numbers.
- ❑ Generate TheBook.pdf.

The process is now demonstrated by example. The example book has these chapter files.

01_Spring.pdf
02_Summer.pdf
03_Fall.pdf
04_Winter.pdf

First, download the latest jPDF Tweak. Click on the OUTPUT tab, and enable the use of temporary files. This is required for books with more than 200 pages, so always enable this option as the default setting.

Now open jPDF Tweak, and identify the input files. Click on the INPUT tab as shown below. Click the box labeled "Multiple file input/Select pages". Click the SELECT button, and select the chapter files by browsing the file directory.

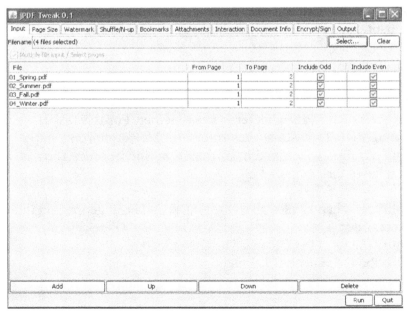

Now identify the output file. Click on the OUTPUT tab as shown below. Browse for the output file path by clicking on the button labeled "...". I recommend the filename TheChapters.pdf.

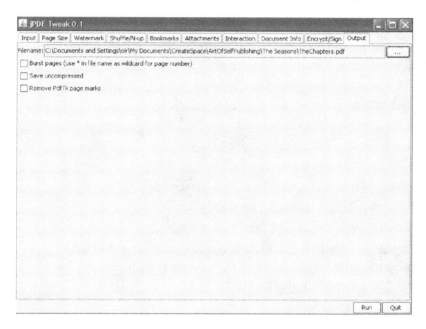

Now configure the font size and position for the page numbers. Click on the WATERMARK tab as shown below. Click on the box labeled "Add page numbers". I recommend font size 9, horizontal 0 points from center, and vertical 25 points from bottom.

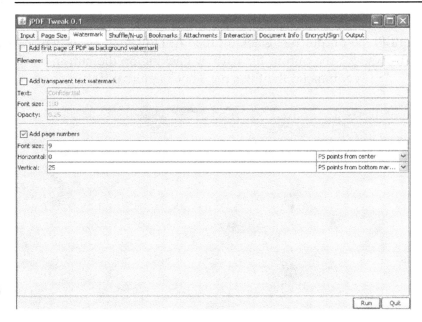

Generate the pdf file that contains the numbered pages of the chapters by clicking the RUN button. You can open this pdf file to make sure things were done correctly.

Page numbers are now in the correct location and sequence. Page numbers are not used for the front pages of the book, so this feature will now be turned off. Click on the WATERMARK tab and uncheck the "Add page numbers" box.

The final step in this assembly process is creation of a single pdf file that contains the whole book. This is the file that will be uploaded to CreateSpace for publication. Define the filename for the pdf file for the whole book. I recommend the name TheBook.pdf. Click on the OUTPUT tab and enter this name. Click on the INPUT tab and enter the name of the two pdf files to stitch together. In this example, this is TheFrontOfBook.pdf and TheChapters.pdf, as shown below.

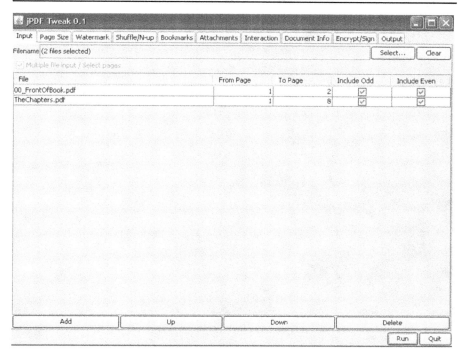

Click the RUN button and generate the pdf book file.

The next step is submitting the book to CreateSpace for publication. You will also need a cover, but we will define a placeholder for the cover when we submit the book, and then put the submission process on hold while the cover is worked on. That seems backwards, but that is the method I have found works best with CreateSpace.

Inspect the pdf file that was just created that contains the interior pages for your book. If the content is correct and the pages have the right style, then your book is print ready. If you have made it to this milestone, then proceed to the next chapter to learn how to use your CreateSpace account.

CreateSpace 101
--- guide to your account

For self-publishing and print-on-demand, CreateSpace is my publisher of choice. CreateSpace is a member of the Amazon group of companies. Through that connection, it is possible to have your book available for sale on-demand in as little as a week. Here are some features of CreateSpace.

- No membership fees (standard program)
- No book setup fees (standard option)
- No print minimums
- Your book is always in stock
- Free tools for content preparation
- CreateSpace ISBN provided at no charge
- Low pricing on author book orders
- Your distribution options are kept open by a non-exclusive agreement
- Connect, collaborate and network with other authors online.
- Build your book cover online using professional templates and customizable themes.

Create your account

Get on the Internet and visit CreateSpace. Create an account. It is easy and takes only a few minutes. At one point in the registration process, you will be asked for your tax ID number. This is usually your Social Security number. This can be left blank for now if you are worried about sharing this information with a service you may decide not to use. Your tax ID is required when your book sales start so that you can be paid. Without your tax ID, your book sale revenue will be withheld.

Dashboard

The dashboard is the user interface for your CreateSpace account. It is here where you add new book titles and manage book content. When you log in to your CreateSpace account, you are taken to the dashboard. To start a book publishing project, click the "Add New Title" button, and select Paperback Book.

After clicking on the "Add New Title" button, a shaded block will be displayed with four tabs.

- ❑ Title Setup
- ❑ File Review
- ❑ Order Proof
- ❑ Print Ready

To create a book that is print ready, you need to complete each of the listed tasks in sequence. You can't submit your book for review until your title setup is complete. You can't order a proof until file review is complete. So let's go through each step in the process, starting with Title Setup.

Title Setup - Title Information
Enter the information for your book. The minimum required entries are

❑ Title - This is the full title of your book.
❑ Description - Prepare a good description of your book so that people can locate it when searching on Amazon. Think of how you have located similar books in the past when searching on Amazon or Google.
❑ ISBN (use the free one assigned by CreateSpace)
❑ Selected BISAC category - Select a category for your book that will be used by Amazon. You are the only person checking that your book is categorized correctly. Do a good job and it will result in better sales.
❑ Authored by

Here is a complete listing of what can be entered in the Title Setup.

* Description
about the description...

You may enter a maximum of 2,000 characters in book description field.

* ISBN
what's this?

◉ Assign my book an ISBN-13/EAN-13 immediately.
IMPORTANT: If you select this option, an ISBN-13/EAN-13 will be immediately assigned to your book upon clicking the Save & Continue button at the bottom of this page. Once the page has been saved, the selection cannot be changed.

○ I already own an ISBN-10 for this book.

This cannot be changed after you submit this book for publishing.

○ I already own an ISBN-13/EAN-13 for this book.

This cannot be changed after you submit this book for publishing.
If you have an ISBN that you purchased from R.R. Bowker or the International ISBN agency specifically for this book, you may use it in publishing your book through our tool. Please note you will be required to also enter an imprint (or publisher) name and that we will verify the ownership and authenticity of the ISBN you enter.

Imprint Name
what's this?

This cannot be changed after you submit this book for publishing.

BISAC Category
what's this?

Enter BISAC Category Code

Add Selected

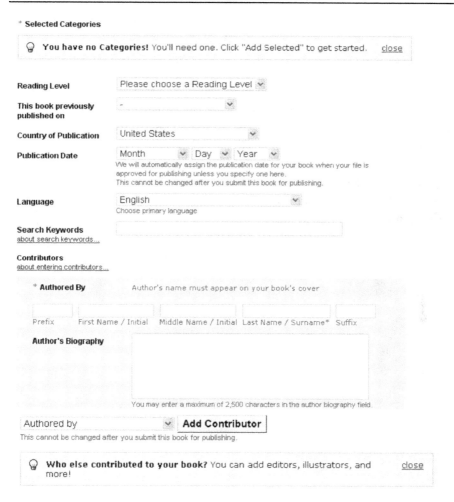

After all information has been entered, press the "Save and Continue" button. If you take too long before saving this page on Title Information, you will need to fill out the form again. If you need to take a break before you are finished with this form, or any of the other forms, click on the "Save and Continue" button. This will save a copy of the form with whatever information you have supplied so far. You can now logout of CreateSpace if you need to and continue later where you left off.

It is important to note that some of the entries cannot be changed after you submit your book for publication. That "point of no return" comes later in the process. It is at least a week away when you reach the Print Ready task. It will be obvious when you are at this decision point because there is wording that reminds you that changes are no longer possible after clicking the approval button. Until you reach that point, you can go back and change anything you have already typed in.

Title Setup - Physical Properties
You need to update the Number of Pages will update each time you upload a revised pdf version of your book.

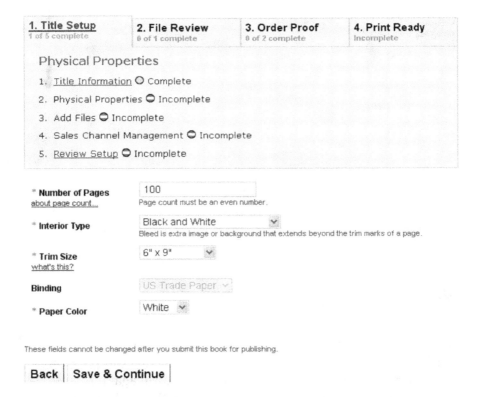

If you are thinking small, you should know that the minimum number of pages is 24. The number of pages is used to compute the publishing price of your book. The number of pages is also used in generating a template for your book cover. The more pages you have, the wider the spine needs to be on the cover artwork.

Select the Interior Type, which in most cases is Black and White. A Picture Book will be in color.

Select the Trim Size and Paper Color. All books I have produced have been 6"x9" on white paper.

Title Setup - Add Files (Interior and Cover)

After entering the title information, upload the interior file. You can design your own cover file and upload it at this point, but I advise beginners to design the cover using one of the great cover templates that CreateSpace supplies.

1. Title Setup	2. File Review	3. Order Proof	4. Print Ready
2 of 5 complete	0 of 1 complete	0 of 2 complete	Incomplete

Add Files

1. Title Information ○ Complete
2. Physical Properties ○ Complete
3. Add Files ◓ Incomplete
4. Sales Channel Management ◓ Incomplete
5. Review Setup ◓ Incomplete

Add your interior and cover files.

According to the interior type and page count you specified on the Physical Properties page, your book's spine width is 0.23 inches.

Your book's ISBN is 1449927823 and EAN-13 is 9781449927820.

Book Interior

You do not currently have an interior file.

Upload a PDF

Format your own book interior file. Read our PDF Submission Requirements.

Download Cover Template

ZIP

Begin download
2mb Compressed Zip File

This Zip file contains

Adobe® Photoshop Template, PNG Template and instructions.

If you have chosen to use the ISBN from CreateSpace, it is now listed on this "Add Files" form.

To upload your pdf version of your pages, click on the "Upload a PDF" button. This is a simple process. Just point to where the book file is located on your computer, and wait for the pdf file to upload to your CreateSpace Account.

Now you can create the cover of your book. Until you have more experience with self-publishing, I recommend using one of the cover templates. This option is the Easy option under the Book Cover section of the form. This option has everything I need for the cover except for one feature. The spine does not contain any wording. With my keep-it-simple approach to self-publishing I can live without the title and my name of the spine. If sales take off for any title I publish, I can always do a revised edition with a custom pdf file for the cover.

Click on the "Create a Cover" button to begin creation of the cover. There are many options available to customize each template, so with minimal effort, you can create a cover that is unique. Here is a picture showing how my cover template looked before any changes were made.

On the right side of the window is a preview of the cover showing front, back, and spine. On the left side of the window is a list of tasks related to the information that appears on the cover, as well as color schemes and artwork. To complete the cover, all eleven tasks need green circles.

One caution on the use of these cover templates. If you change the theme, you will lose many of the custom selections you have already made. To avoid doing the same tasks more than once, explore the unmodified templates library. Select a theme that best fits your book before you start making any changes to it.

Title Setup: Sales Channel Management

Create Space will tell you how much it will cost you to produce a copy of your book. From this, you can set the list price for your book. The list price will determine the royalty you make through each sales channel. You also decide which sales channel to use for your book. I recommend selling your book through both Amazon.com and the CreateSpace E-Store. There is also an optional Pro Plan you may purchase which will return more of the sales dollars to you. This form also lists the reduced price of your book to you when you purchase direct from CreateSpace.

Purchasing direct from CreateSpace allows you to market your book through alternative sales channels at a low cost. For example,

41

imagine that you own a small farm, and you sell berries directly to customers at a farmer's market. You decide to self-publish a recipe book for your fruit that compliments berry sales. You can purchase copies of your book direct from CreateSpace that avoids the fee that Amazon charges for purchases made through the on-line store. You should note that this business model is no longer print-on-demand, and you will have a printed book inventory to manage.

Purchasing direct from CreateSpace is also a great deal for books you will give as gifts. If you plan on distributing a few books to book reviewers as part of your marketing campaign, you should also purchase those directly to keep your expenses low.

With the interior pages of the book uploaded and the cover of the book designed, it is time to make a business decision. How much will you sell your book for? What should you enter for the List Price for the Sales Channel Management section of the Title Setup? It should be no surprise that sales will be low if you set the price too high, but your profit will be low if you set the price too low.

You can get an idea of what price the market will bear by looking at what similar books are selling for. Amazon does not list how many copies of each title have sold, but you can get an idea by looking at Sales Rank numbers. Dog Ear Publishing has a web page devoted to Amazon Sales Rank. What they have done is post Sales Rank numbers for some of the titles they publish along with the actual weekly sales for those same titles.

Sales Rank	Weekly Sales
1,000	90 copies
10,000	60 copies
100,000	16 copies
300,000	12 copies
500,000	1 copy
1,000,000	1 copy per month

This relation between Amazon Sales Rank and weekly sales is not exact. The rate of change in sales is also a factor in the rank. If two titles sell the same number of copies in a week, but title A is rising in popularity while title B is fading, then title A would receive the higher rank. Only Amazon knows the secret sauce for computing sales rank. The rest of us can only speculate on what goes into it. The reason I think it is a good idea to study the Sales Rank of similar titles is that it gives you feel for how popular your book will be a different price points.

Here is an example of how I use Amazon Sales Rank to set the list price of my book. For anyone who has bought or sold a house, you may see a similarity with appraising the value of a house. First I find three titles that are similar to my book. I write down the list price and the rank for each title. I have often found that the book with the lower list price will have a better rank. Next I look at the table of Sales Rank and Weekly Sales. I then compare the Sales Rank numbers for the three titles and get an estimate of how many books I can sell each week at the different price points. If I'm confident that my book will be better than the competition, then I set a higher price. If I think my potential buyer are more concerned about price than difference in content to similar books, then I will price my book lower. How much profit is enough for you? I have not seen any formula for this. Setting the price is more of an art than a science. By doing this comparison you at least won't be totally in the dark about what a good List Price would be.

As long as we are on the topic of Sales Rank, another use I have found for this number is in the selection of the title for my book. I brainstorm titles, writing down a list of candidates. I then search Amazon for books with similar titles. I have found that certain words or phrases in titles result in high sales, while others lead to poor sales. It is like certain words scare away potential customers. A good title can generate interest in your book, but your title still needs to reflect what the your book's content. The Amazon Sales Rank can give you insight into what titles may work best for your book, so give it a try.

Title Setup: Review Setup
If you have made it this far, you are now ready to submit your book for review. Create Space will notify you via email when your files have been approved, usually within 24 hours. If you have errors with your files, fix them. If there are no corrections required, then order a proof.

Review Setup

1. Title Information ○ Complete
2. Physical Properties ○ Complete
3. Add Files ○ Complete
4. Sales Channel Management ○ Complete
5. Review Setup ○ Incomplete

Title Information (Complete) Edit

Title ID	3413851
Title	Mastering the Art of Self-Publishing
Subtitle	Amazon, CreateSpace and your book project
Description	This guide will take you step-by-step through the self-publishing process using CreateSpace. Start selling your book on-line through Amazon in as quick as one week. Produce your own professional quali...
ISBN	1449927823
EAN-13	9781449927820
Primary Category	Computers / Desktop Applications / Desktop Publishing
Country of Publication	United States
Language	English
Search Keywords	self-publish;createspace;amazon;kindle
Contributors	*Authored by* Mark Robert Lee

Physical Properties (Complete) Edit

Number of Pages	52
Interior Type	Black and White
Trim Size	6" x 9"
Binding	US Trade Paper
Paper Color	White

Add Files (Complete) Edit

Book Interior   TheBook.pdf Nov 30 2009
Book Cover

Nov 30 2009

Sales Channel Management (Complete) Edit

Pro	No
List Price	$ X.XX
Sell via Amazon Retail Sales	Yes
Amazon Retail Sales status	Requested
Sell via E-Store Sales	Yes
Type of E-Store	Public
Sales Region	US and international sales

History View

3 items found, displaying all items.

Creation Date	Subject
Nov 30 2009	Cover File Update on Book #3413851
Nov 30 2009	Interior File Update on Book #3413851
Nov 30 2009	Interior File Update on Book #3413851

Save & Continue

At this point, the wording on the Review Setup page is a little confusing. Clicking on the "Submit for Publishing" means you are submitting your interior pages of your book for a Dimensional Rule Check. When you click on the "Save and Continue" button, you are requesting that CreateSpace review the book to see if it meets the requirements for printing and binding with the Print-on-Demand printing press. "Submit for Publishing" does not mean you are going live with Amazon book sales, or that you are ordering a proof copy. Those steps come later. After clicking the submit button, you will see the confirmation screen shown below. It has some important wording. Note that you will not have access to the files and information you have entered for the next 24 to 48 hours while the review is taking place.

If you have some changes to your cover that you can't wait to make, do them now before you click on the submit button. Once you click the "Submit for Publishing" button, your CreateSpace project is on hold until the review is complete. Go find something else to do for the next day or two. One time my book was reviewed in two hours. That was a pleasant surprise. It may happen this fast for you, but don't count on it.

File Review

After you click the "Submit for Publishing" button, you can check the status of the review process here. There is nothing for you to do other than wait.

The result of the review will either be that it is accepted, or that changes are required. If you have changes to make, go back to the Title Setup tab and make the changes. When the changes are complete, submit the book again for review. When the book is accepted, then you can order a proof copy. That takes place on the next tab.

Order Proof

There are three steps involved in the Order Proof section. The first step is placing an order for the proof copy. The second step is a review of the proof copy by you and you book reading friends after the copy arrives in the mail. The third step is your approval of the proof copy needing no further corrections

The process of ordering a proof copy is similar to the way you order any book through an online bookstore. You fill a virtual shopping cart with your order and then give your shipping information and your credit card number. You specify where you want it shipped, how you are paying for it, and how fast you want it. You will only pay for production costs of printing the book and for shipping. Once your book sales go live through Amazon, you will pay a fee to Amazon for each copy, but for ordering proof copies of your book, that fee is waived.

| 1. Title Setup | 2. File Review | 3. Order Proof | 4. Print Ready |
| Complete | Complete | 1 of 2 complete | Incomplete |

Proof Review

1. Order Proof
2. Proof Review

Approve Proof

Title Information (Complete) Edit

Title ID	3413851
Title	Mastering the Art of Self-Publishing
Subtitle	Amazon, CreateSpace and your book project
Description	This guide will take you step-by-step through the self-publishing process using CreateSpace. Start selling your book on-line through Amazon in as quick as one week. Produce your own professional quali...
ISBN	1449927823
EAN-13	9781449927820
Primary Category	Computers / Desktop Applications / Desktop Publishing
Country of Publication	United States
Language	English
Search Keywords	self-publish;createspace;amazon;kindle
Contributors	*Authored by* Mark Lee

When your proof arrives, what do you check for? There is a checklist at the end of this book. Go through that list and make sure that everything looks OK. If you have changes to make, you need to go back to the Title Setup. If the proof is ready to sell as-is, then click on the "Approve Proof" button.

Print Ready

After click on the "Approve Proof" button, your book will soon appear for sale on Amazon. The final tab is now display on the dashboard of your book project. It shows you that the book is available for sale. It also will show you what your books will cost you if you buy directly through your dashboard shopping cart.

1. Title Setup	2. File Review	3. Order Proof	4. Print Ready
Complete	Complete	Complete	Complete

Purchase Ready

Use the edit links below to update your title's information.

Book Availability

Your title is currently **Available**
Placing your title "On Hold" will stop sales and production of your title. Place your title On Hold

Order Copies of your Book

Upgrade your Publishing Plan!

☐ Standard **$X.XX each** | Buy Now |

Keep more of each sale of this book and pay less when you order copies by going Pro! Learn More

▣ Pro **$X.XX each**

☆ **Pro** Plan **$ XX.XX** | Upgrade |

Go to Amazon.com and find your book. The Amazon page has a thumbnail view of the front cover and a place for reviews of the book. Note that the book is always in stock. CreateSpace books are print-on-demand, so Amazon lists that books are always ready to ship.

Example Timeline

You may be wondering how long the whole process takes. Here is an example as recorded in the Message Center of my CreateSpace account. The first manuscript was submitted October 5 and appeared for sale on Amazon on October 13. This is a total of 8 days from start to finish. Here is the detailed timeline.

Oct 5   Confirmation of account setup.
Oct 5   Upload interior file - complete.
Oct 5   Cover design - complete.
Oct 6   Upload revised interior file.
Oct 6   Submit book for review.
Oct 6   Review complete. No changes required.
Oct 6   Order proof copy.
Oct 9   Proof copy arrives in mail. No changes required.
Oct 9   Proof copy approved. E-Store goes live.
Oct 13   Book appears for sale on Amazon.

This chapter showed how to use your CreateSpace account to get your book published. The next chapter takes a short look at marketing your book.

That's my book on Amazon!
--- marketing your book

After approving the proof copy you received in the mail, your book sales will go live on Amazon and your CreateSpace E-Store. So once the writing is complete, and the book is published, your self-publishing activity quickly transitions from writing and page layout to book marketing and tracking sales. Here is a look at some of the marketing tools available to you through your CreateSpace account.

Managing sales through the CreateSpace Dashboard
Once your book is available both in the E-Store and on Amazon.com, you can track your sales through your Create Space Dashboard. The Dashboard was briefly introduced earlier in this book. It was shown how to start a book project with CreateSpace by clicking on the "Add Title" button. Now that your book project has entered the sales and marketing phase, it is time to revisit this part of your CreateSpace account. Through the Dashboard, you can track the following sales numbers for all your titles.

Title Name - The title of your book.
Title ID - Number assigned by CreateSpace.
Status - Available (on Amazon), Proof Ready, etc.
List Price - The price you set for customers.
Units Sold - Total sales through Amazon and E-Store
Royalties - The money you keep from all sales.

The Dashboard presents four icons for each book project you have. Clicking on an icon takes you to another webpage where you can perform one of the essential sales management tasks.

Edit Title - This sounds like the icon to click on if you want to change the name of your book. Ironically, this is one thing you can't do from this icon. The "title" in this case is another name for your book project. By clicking on the "Edit Title" icon you can access the Title Setup page. After your book has been approved for publication and sales go live, it is not possible to change the name of the book, or the physical size of the book. You can always place your sales on hold if you ever need to make a major change like that, but that is not the main use of the "Edit Title" icon. After your book sales go live, you click on the "Edit Title" icon if you need to edit your E-Store set-up, change your list price, create discounts for your customers on Amazon, or recall the history of your book project.

View Sales Report - Detailed sales report for each title. Numbers are reported for Units Sold and Royalties. Units Sold are broken out into the categories of Proofs, Amazon, E-Store and Sales to the Author. Royalties are listed out per channel (Amazon and E-Store). You can also configure automatic delivery of the sales report via e-mail from this page.

Visit E-Store - Click on this icon to go to the E-Store for your book.

Order a Copy - Buy copies of your book at the special author price.

Your E-store Sales Channel
CreateSpace gives you an E-Store for free. This is a fully functioning e-commerce site dedicated to sales of your book. By steering people to your E-Store, you will keep more of the purchase price in your pocket. You can customize your E-Store colors to reflect the subject matter of your book. You also have the option of adding your own banner and promotional clips.

The screenshot above shows a view of a typical E-Store. When the customer clicks on the "Add to Cart" button, they are taken to a shopping cart page showing quantity ordered, a "proceed to checkout" button, etc. The customer then enters shipping and billing information, and checks-out. This is a full bookstore e-commerce application dedicated to this one title. Each book project you maintain on CreateSpace has its own E-Store.

When customers purchase your book through your E-Store instead of Amazon, you will keep more of the list price. So how do you steer customers to the E-Store? To direct customers to your store, you need to give them the address. The address for your E-Store is https://www.createspace.com/"Title ID". You can get the Title ID on the Dashboard. You can also find the complete URL for the address through your Dashboard by clicking on the book title on the Dashboard, and scrolling down to the E-Store section.

Why would your customers purchase through your E-Store instead of from Amazon? There is only one list price used by both Amazon and your E-Store, so there is no price advantage. But you can reduce the price for your E-Store customers using a discount. If you decide that offering a discount makes sense for your book, here is how you do it. When you promote your book, whenever you give the link to your E-Store, also share a discount code. You can also list the discount code right on the E-Store. Give the customer back some of the extra money you gain through your E-Store sales, and you may shift more of your sales to your higher value E-Store. Any discounts you offer can be used equally in the E-Store and on Amazon, so give your discount a title like "E-Store Customer Loyalty Discount" and your customers are more likely to use it with your E-Store. That's called marketing.

To setup a discount, click on the book title on the Dashboard and scroll down to discounts, and click the Edit link. On the Discounts page, create a discount code by clicking on "Click here". You will receive an 8-digit discount code. You can generate multiple discount codes, so decide which one of them will apply to each book you have. Also decide whether the discount type is a dollar amount or a percentage amount, and then enter the amount assigned to the discount. Complete the process by clicking on the "Save Changes" button.

E-store makes sense if you maintain your own website, and you want customers to click through to your own e-commerce site to buy a book. When the customer leaves your other website and goes to the E-Store, you may need to customize your E-Store to smooth that transition. To customize the E-Store, go to the Dashboard and click on the Book Title link. You can add a banner to your store. Banner size has limits. Banner max height is 200 pixels, and width min is 570 pixels. If you load a banner, it is at the top of all your E-Store pages - shopping cart, shipping billing, etc, so it is should be something simple like a logo and a slogan that is associated with your other website. You can go crazy changing colors, but I recommend sticking with a white background for your store. Keep it simple. A white background works for Amazon, and they sell a lot of book, so that seems like a good model to go with. Definitely don't use background image - too busy. Payment through your store is handled through a 3rd party e-commerce site that processes credit cards. Be aware that the registration process for using this service takes the customer to yet another website, but at least the look and feel of your E-Store are maintained in this process.

Your Amazon Sales Channel

After approving the proof copy you received in the mail, book sales start immediately through the E-Store, but you may have to wait up to fifteen business days for your book to go live on Amazon.com. You need to be patient. Remember that your main investment in this process is time. Before print-on-demand services and CreateSpace, the only way to get your book onto Amazon was the traditional publishing route. That involved either putting up your own money to print the book yourself, or printing the book through a publisher if they think your title has a big enough market. For writers just starting out, the traditional route to Amazon sales is a steep barrier. Now through CreateSpace, all you have to do is jump through a few hoops and wait.

When your book appears for sale on Amazon, try searching for it by title. When you go to the page for the book, note that the book is "in stock". Your book will always be in stock since it is print on demand.

Wait another week and you should see a "Look Inside" feature showing up for your book. This allows customers to preview a few pages of your book.

Two items on the Amazon page have the potential to increase your sales - the book description, and the book review.

Read over the description. Does the wording you entered earlier in the process still make sense? If you knew nothing about your book, do you want to buy it after reading the description? If your description needs work, go to your Title Setup page on your CreateSpace account and make the changes.

As with all books on Amazon, your book will have a spot for reviews. Sometimes reviews show up on their own, other times you need to do some prodding. To get the ball rolling, give the book to a friend and ask for a review, and then follow up with the reminder to enter the review.

This completes the self-publishing process. Hopefully all that hard work will pay off for you. Welcome to the world of Self-Publishing.

Kindle-ing
--- e-book sales

E-book reader sales are growing each year. As more people routinely use their readers while passing time on their daily commute or relaxing in a coffee shop, the demand for e-book titles is on the rise. The Kindle from Amazon is one of the most popular e-book readers. If you have a manuscript that is ready to go, it takes little effort to start selling your title through the Kindle Store. Since no physical book needs to be produced for you to review a proof copy of your title, it is even cheaper to start selling your book through the Kindle Store compared to the already low entry fee of Amazon sales with CreateSpace. How much cheaper? It's free.

If you have already gone through the work of creating a physical book with CreateSpace, take a little more time and give e-book sales a try. So here is how to start selling your book in the e-book format through the Kindle Store.

Log in to your DTP dashboard
Like the CreateSpace dashboard where you manage traditional book sales of your book on Amazon, the sales of your e-book through the Kindle Store are managed through the Digital Text Platform dashboard. DTP is shorthand for Digital Text Platform. If you have an active account on Amazon that you use to make online purchases, then you can log in to your DTP dashboard without any additional work. Go to the address http://www.digitaltextplatform.com and log in. If you don't have an account on Amazon, or you want to have a

separate account for e-book sales, then create a new DTP account at the same address. Go to the "My Account" tab of the dashboard and enter your account details so you can receive payment for your e-book sales.

Add a new book project to your dashboard

Start a new book project by clicking on the "Add new item" button on the dashboard.

Enter the product details

Click on the "Enter Product Details" button. Enter information in the required fields: Title, Author, Language, and Categories. Filling out the Description field should also be mandatory since this is how a potential buyer of your e-book will know that your book contains the information they are searching for. After reading a good description, the reader will think, "I have to get that book".

Confirm content rights

Next, click on the "Confirm Content Rights" button. If your work is original, you can publish it anywhere. If this is the case, then select "Worldwide rights- all territories". If for some reason you have limited rights for selling your e-book, then select the territories that apply.

Upload the book

After your book is uploaded, it is converted to a format that is readable by Kindle. Amazon states that HTML format is the most compatible with the conversion process. Other compatible formats are pdf, plain text (txt), and Microsoft Word (doc). Browse for the location of your book file and click the "Upload" button.

Preview the book

After automated conversion of your book to the Kindle format, you will receive confirmation from DTP. At this point you need to preview your book, which is the electronic equivalent of paging through a physical proof copy. Make any corrections that are required and upload your book again.

Set the list price

You set the list price of your book on the Kindle Store. The price range is $0.99 to $200. You will receive a set percentage of this list price for each e-book sale. The percentage is defined in the Amazon DTP Terms and Conditions.

Publish the book

Once you have made all required changes, click the "Publish" button. It will take 24 to 72 hours for your title to first appear in the Kindle Store. When your e-book first goes live, some of the product details you entered may be missing. It may take up to a week for the Kindle Store page for your e-book to be complete.

Get paid for your e-book sales

The Kindle Store is invoice-free. You are paid by Electronic Funds Transfer to a U.S. bank account. Besides a U.S. bank account, you also need a U.S. social security number (SSN) or taxpayer identification number (TIN) to receive payment from Amazon DTP. This information must be supplied through Account Details section of your dashboard before payment can be received. Payments are made automatically, but not immediately after each sale. The delay in payment can be up to 3 months. The official wording is "sixty days following the end of the calendar month during which the applicable sales of your content occur". When a sale is made, your account accumulates a percentage of the list price as defined in the Amazon DTP Terms and Conditions. Here is an example of how payment works. Let's say you earn $1.50 for each e-book you sell. In January you sell 100 copies. Your dashboard will show that you are owed $150 for January sales. Around the end of March you will receive an Electronic Funds Transfer to your U.S. bank account in the amount of $150.

You can find out more about e-book sales and your DTP account through the DTP Forums and Knowledgebase.

Best of luck to you as you begin to master the art of self-publishing.

Self-Publisher's Checklist

Start your project - Unformatted text files

❑ Sketch out your thoughts (paper and pencil).
❑ Organize major topics into chapters.
❑ Use simple text files until manuscript is 80-90% complete.
❑ One text file per chapter using any text editor (Notepad).
❑ Recommend file names start with chapter number. If chapter 1 is about the season of Spring, then use name 01_spring.txt.
❑ Use placeholder for illustrations, <picture goes here>

Formatted Word files - The Style

❑ *Microsoft Word* recommended for word processing (Word file).
❑ Each chapter has even number of pages.
❑ If text fills odd number of pages, add blank page for even total.
❑ Unique style for left page, right pages, and first page of chapter.
❑ First page of chapter always on right side of the spine.
❑ Pages on left side of spine have book title in header.
❑ Pages on right side of spine have chapter title in header.
❑ First page of chapter does not have header.
❑ No page numbers in formatted Word files.

Formatted Word files – The Chapters

- ❏ Change filename from *.txt to *.doc.
- ❏ No page numbers.
- ❏ The "left" pages have own header with book title.
- ❏ "Left" page header called "Even Page Header" in Word.
- ❏ The "right" pages have own header with book title.
- ❏ "Right" page header called "Odd Page Header" in Word.
- ❏ First page of a chapter is a "right" page, inner margin on the left.
- ❏ First page of the chapter has own header. It is left blank.

Formatted Word files – Front of Book

- ❏ Filename = 00_FrontOfBook.doc
- ❏ No page numbers, no header or footer.
- ❏ Page order: Title Page, Copyright Page, Contents
- ❏ Optional page order: Half Title Page, Facing Page, Title Page, Copyright Page, Dedication, Blank Page, Contents, Preface, Acknowledgements
- ❏ Copyright is secured when work is created. No publication is required. Copyright registration is optional.
- ❏ Copyright Page: Copyright © [year] [author name]
- ❏ Copyright Page: Include wording "All rights reserved..."
- ❏ Copyright Page: ISBN numbers
- ❏ Copyright Page: Printed in [country]
- ❏ Contents: Generate Table of Contents manually
- ❏ Contents: List chapter titles and placeholder page numbers.

Convert Word files to PDF files – Chapters

- ❏ *doPDF* is recommended for converting Word files to PDF.
- ❏ Select "Embed Fonts" option when generating PDF file.
- ❏ Chapters: Create one PDF file for every Word file.
- ❏ Chapters: Filename = XX-Chaptername.pdf
- ❏ Chapters: No page numbers for individual chapter files.

Stitch together PDF files - Page Numbers

- ❑ *jPDF Tweak* is recommended for merging PDF files.
- ❑ Chapters: Identify the chapter files as INPUT files, and arrange them in the correct order.
- ❑ Chapters: Identify the OUTPUT file as TheChapters.pdf.
- ❑ Chapters: Define the placement of the page numbers.
- ❑ Chapters: Enable the placement of page numbers.
- ❑ Chapters: Generate TheChapters.pdf.
- ❑ Contents: Record correct page numbers for first page of each Chapter.
- ❑ Contents: Open 00_FrontOfBook.doc, place correct page numbers into Table of Contents placeholders.

Convert Word -> PDF - Front of Book

- ❑ Front of Book: Convert Word file to PDF.
- ❑ Front of Book: Filename = 00_FrontOfBook.pdf.
- ❑ Front of Book: Disable the placement of page numbers.

Stitch together PDF files - Whole Book

- ❑ Use *jPDF Tweak* again.
- ❑ Book: Identify two files as the new INPUT files, TheFrontOfBook.pdf and TheChapters.pdf.
- ❑ Book: Identify the new OUTPUT file as TheBook.pdf.
- ❑ Book: Disable the placement of new page numbers.
- ❑ Book: Generate TheBook.pdf.

Order the proof

- ❑ Create account on CreateSpace
- ❑ Select category for Amazon Sales (BISAC category).
- ❑ Select trim size (e.g. 6" x 9").
- ❑ Create cover using CreateSpace template.
- ❑ Set list price.
- ❑ Submit book for review.
- ❑ Order Proof.

Inspecting the proof

- ❏ Text on front cover.
- ❏ Text on back cover.
- ❏ Text of Chapter Titles
- ❏ Chapter Title placement
- ❏ First page of chapters on Right Page.
- ❏ No header on first page of chapters.
- ❏ Header: Book Title on Left Page.
- ❏ Header: Chapter Title on Right Page.
- ❏ Title Page text.
- ❏ Copyright Page text.
- ❏ Contents: Chapter Title text.
- ❏ Contents: Page numbers.
- ❏ Front of Book: No page numbers.
- ❏ Front of Book: No header.
- ❏ Chapters: Page number placement.
- ❏ Chapters: Page number font.
- ❏ Chapters: Text font style and font size.
- ❏ Margins on all pages.
- ❏ No typos.
- ❏ Illustrations the right size and good quality.

Start selling your book on Amazon

- ❏ Approve the proof.
- ❏ Check for your book on your CreateSpace E-Store.
- ❏ Check for your book on Amazon.
- ❏ Monitor sales on your CreateSpace account Dashboard.

E-book sales using Kindle Store

- ❏ Log in to your DTP dashboard
- ❏ Add a new book project to your dashboard
- ❏ Enter the product details
- ❏ Confirm content rights
- ❏ Upload the book
- ❏ Preview the book
- ❏ Set the list price
- ❏ Publish the book
- ❏ Get paid for your e-book sales